Origins

Foolish Fears

Richard Platt
Illustrations by Paul Moran

Contents

What are you frightened of?	2
Superstition	4
Dreams and nightmares	8
Scary monsters	10
Alien invaders	12
Light and dark	14
The Sun eaten up	16
Fear of the dark	18
Your destiny in the stars	20
Stars with fiery tails	22
Mother nature and angry gods	24
What doesn't kill you makes you stronger	26
Bad smells and disease	28
The edge of the Earth	30
Strange people, strange lands	32
Foolishly fast?	34
Can fear be helpful?	36
Future fears	38
Glossary	39
Index	40

OXFORD
UNIVERSITY PRESS

What are you frightened of?

Even the bravest people suffer some fear, for truly dangerous things are genuinely scary. We'd all be frightened if we had to cross a swirling river on a narrow log, or if we were being chased by a fearsome tiger.

But many of us also have 'foolish' fears, of things that cannot really harm us: mice, for example, are not usually deadly and making a speech isn't dangerous – but both can seem quite terrifying!

Ask your friends …
"What are you most scared of?"
- What are the most common answers?
- Are they truly dangerous things, or 'foolish' fears?

Gripped by fear

In the past, foolish fears have been known to seize whole families, towns and even nations. They have been known to make people take unwise decisions: for example, some historians believe that in the year 1000, huge numbers of Europeans sold their possessions and left their homes because they believed the world was about to be destroyed. Today we know they had nothing to fear but, at the time, their terror was very real. To find out more about the foolish fears of our **ancestors**, keep reading.

Fear and phobia

We may laugh at the foolish fears of the past but many of us also have fears we cannot control or explain. A fear of harmless things is called a phobia. Some phobias are very common, such as a fear of spiders or high places. Other people have more unusual phobias, such as *coulrophobia*, a fear of clowns. Although phobias can seem silly to those who don't suffer from them, they can ruin lives. For instance, *agoraphobia*, a fear of open spaces, stops many sufferers from going outdoors.

Name that fear

The names we give to phobias often come from the ancient languages of Latin and Greek. *Agoraphobia* draws on the Greek word *agora*, which means a wide, open marketplace. Can you guess what these phobias are?

There's nothing foolish about my arachnophobia!

chromophobia

dentophobia

zoophobia

bibliophobia

frigophobia

hippophobia

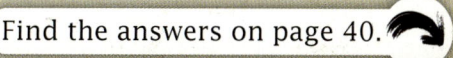
Find the answers on page 40.

Superstition

Don't tread on cracks! Knock on wood! Cross your fingers!

When people fear that terrible things might happen, they often take special steps which they believe will make everything work out well. These steps are called superstitions, a way of thinking that can be traced back to ancient beliefs. But in reality can these actions really change anything?

Fear factor

Superstitions often affect sportspeople. Some footballers have been known to miss the start of matches because their superstitious routines have been disrupted.

Are pigeons superstitious?

In a famous experiment in the 1940s, American scientist Fred Skinner put hungry pigeons in a feeding box. A timer delivered food pellets regularly, no matter what the pigeons did. However, he found that each pigeon linked the food delivery to the action they were doing when the first pellet arrived. They repeated that same 'lucky' action over and over, even though it was the timer and not the action that made the food appear. Skinner said this was like some superstitious human habits.

I told you juggling would do the trick!

Proving it works

Like Skinner's pigeons, superstitious people may notice each time their lucky action 'works' the way they expect, but forget when it doesn't. For example sports stars who have lost after forgetting to wear their 'lucky' clothes have claimed that this proves a superstition works. A more likely explanation is that, just before competing, they realize that they have forgotten them. This upsets them enough to spoil their game.

> " I'm very superstitious. Before a race I go through exactly the same routine ... eight arm swings, four goggle presses, four cap touches. It looks weird but it's become second nature now. "
>
> Australian swimmer Stephanie Rice, interviewed by CNN just before competing in the London Olympics in 2012.

What makes us superstitious?

When something good or bad happens to us, we try to figure out why. Did we see, do or say something different? Is there anything we can control that might make a good thing happen, or stop a bad thing from happening again? We find it easier to blame an action or object that has no real connection to our fortune or misfortune, than to accept that it happened by chance.

Would you care to quaff some of my delectable water?

Truth behind the fear

Some superstitions lead to sensible actions. For example, the superstition that it is unlucky for two people to drink from the same cup may have begun because sharing a drink could spread germs.

Turn the page to read about how other superstitions may have started.

Are you curious about how superstitions started? Here are the origins of some of the most popular ones.

Walking under a ladder

A ladder, its shadow and the wall it leans against make a triangle. In Ancient Egypt, walking underneath a ladder was considered unlucky because it 'broke' the triangle. You also ran the risk of the ladder-user dropping something on your head, of course!

Sneezing

People often say 'Bless you!' when someone sneezes, to ward off bad luck. Some people think this dates back to the plague (see page 28), when sneezing was a symptom of this deadly disease.

The number 13

This number is thought to be unlucky. The Ancient Greeks believed that if 13 people were in a room, one would die. It may have begun because 13 is a **prime number**. Some people believe these numbers are especially lucky – or unlucky. Even today, many hotels don't have a 13th floor.

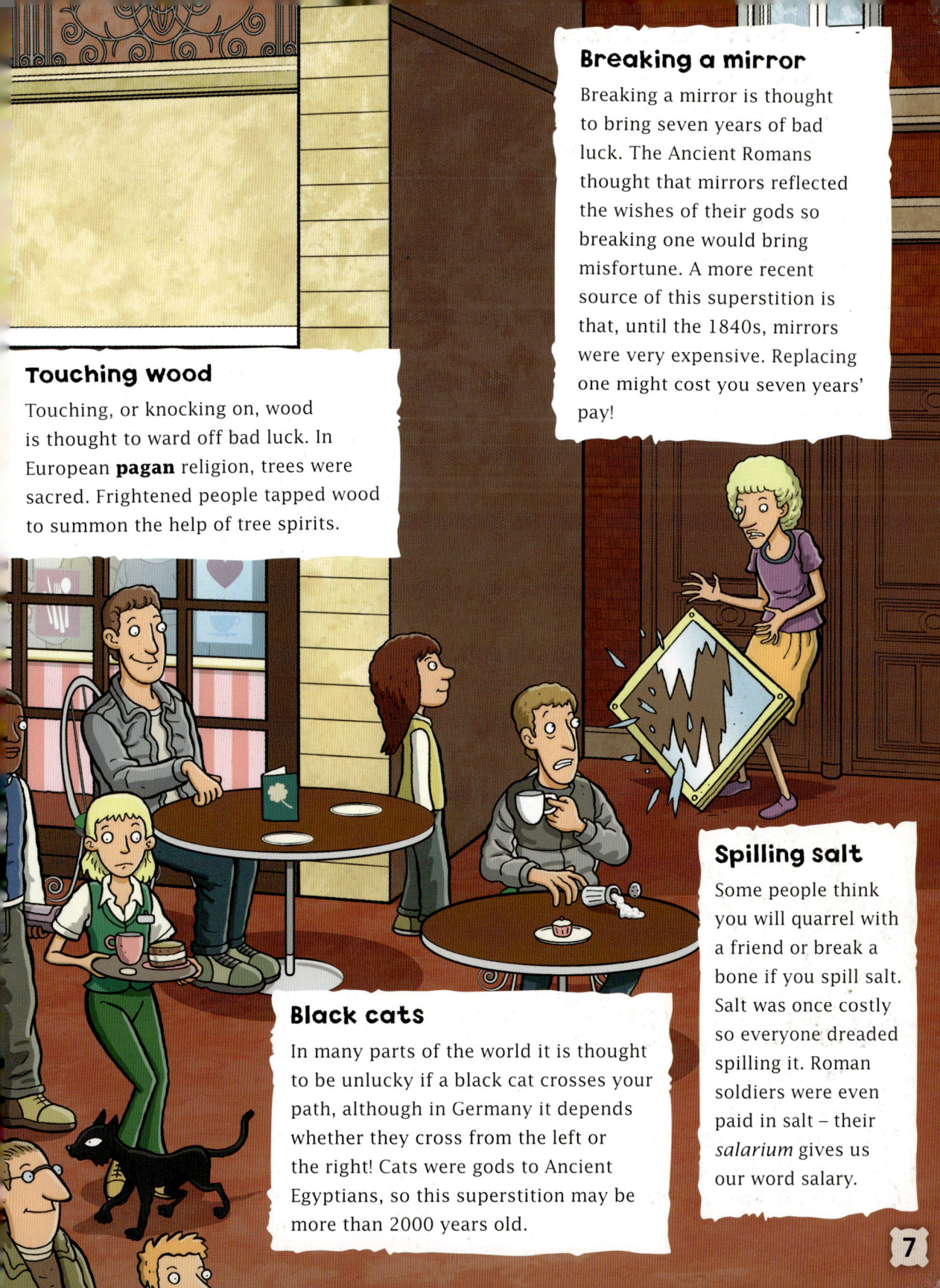

Breaking a mirror

Breaking a mirror is thought to bring seven years of bad luck. The Ancient Romans thought that mirrors reflected the wishes of their gods so breaking one would bring misfortune. A more recent source of this superstition is that, until the 1840s, mirrors were very expensive. Replacing one might cost you seven years' pay!

Touching wood

Touching, or knocking on, wood is thought to ward off bad luck. In European **pagan** religion, trees were sacred. Frightened people tapped wood to summon the help of tree spirits.

Spilling salt

Some people think you will quarrel with a friend or break a bone if you spill salt. Salt was once costly so everyone dreaded spilling it. Roman soldiers were even paid in salt – their *salarium* gives us our word salary.

Black cats

In many parts of the world it is thought to be unlucky if a black cat crosses your path, although in Germany it depends whether they cross from the left or the right! Cats were gods to Ancient Egyptians, so this superstition may be more than 2000 years old.

Dreams and Nightmares

We might be able to control foolish fears that take hold in the daytime but what about frights that invade our minds at night? Nightmares don't seem scary when we're awake but when we're fast asleep they can feel totally real – and totally terrifying.

Fright night

Nightmares scare us because we can't stop or control what's happening in our sleep. In the past, the horror didn't end when the dreamer woke up: people believed that dreams were warnings or glimpses of the future. They worried that a bad dream foretold a bad event in their life.

The president dreams of his death

In April 1865, US president Abraham Lincoln told his wife about a terrifying dream:

> *There seemed to be a death-like stillness about me. Then I heard subdued sobs, as if people were weeping. I left my bed and went from room to room determined to find the cause until I arrived at the East Room. There I met with a sickening surprise. Before me was a corpse wrapped in funeral **vestments**. Around it were stationed soldiers, acting as guards. "Who is dead in the White House?" I demanded. "The president," was his answer; "He was killed by an **assassin**."*

Just a few days later, a man shot President Lincoln dead.

Death is common in dreams because it's something we all fear. It was just a coincidence that Lincoln's death followed his bad dream. However, some superstitious people would still argue that the president's story is proof of the power of dreams.

What are dreams?

Studying dreams is hard. Researchers can't wake up their subjects to ask questions because that would end the dream! Most scientists think that sleep makes us remember random thoughts and events from our own lives, mixed up with things we've read or seen on TV. The thinking part of our brain then tries to make sense of this jumble of ideas, often stitching them together in strange and scary ways.

We fear the same things

Ask your friends about their worst dreams and you'll find that some themes are very common. How often do these come up?

- dying or being injured
- forgetting your clothes
- being chased or running away
- being trapped or getting lost
- failing a test
- falling

Worries creep in

Often nightmares are linked to anxiety. If you go to bed worried, you are likely to dream about whatever is on your mind. In some dreams – such as exam nightmares – the link between the dream and the worry is clear. But why would you dream about being lost in a strange city? Perhaps this is because in real life you have to make important decisions and you are not sure which choice is best. Your dream changes the choices you have to make into different roads and you cannot decide which way to go.

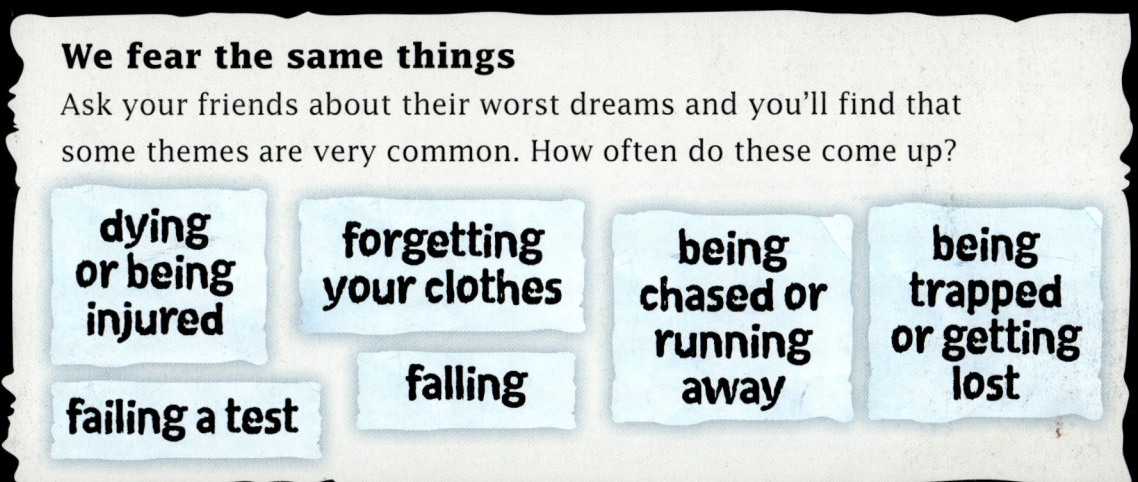

SCARY MONSTERS

Throughout history, people have feared scary-looking creatures with superhuman powers. Though these monsters take many different forms, similar creatures can be found in the legends of distant countries. Just take a look at dragons – these are a common monster throughout the world.

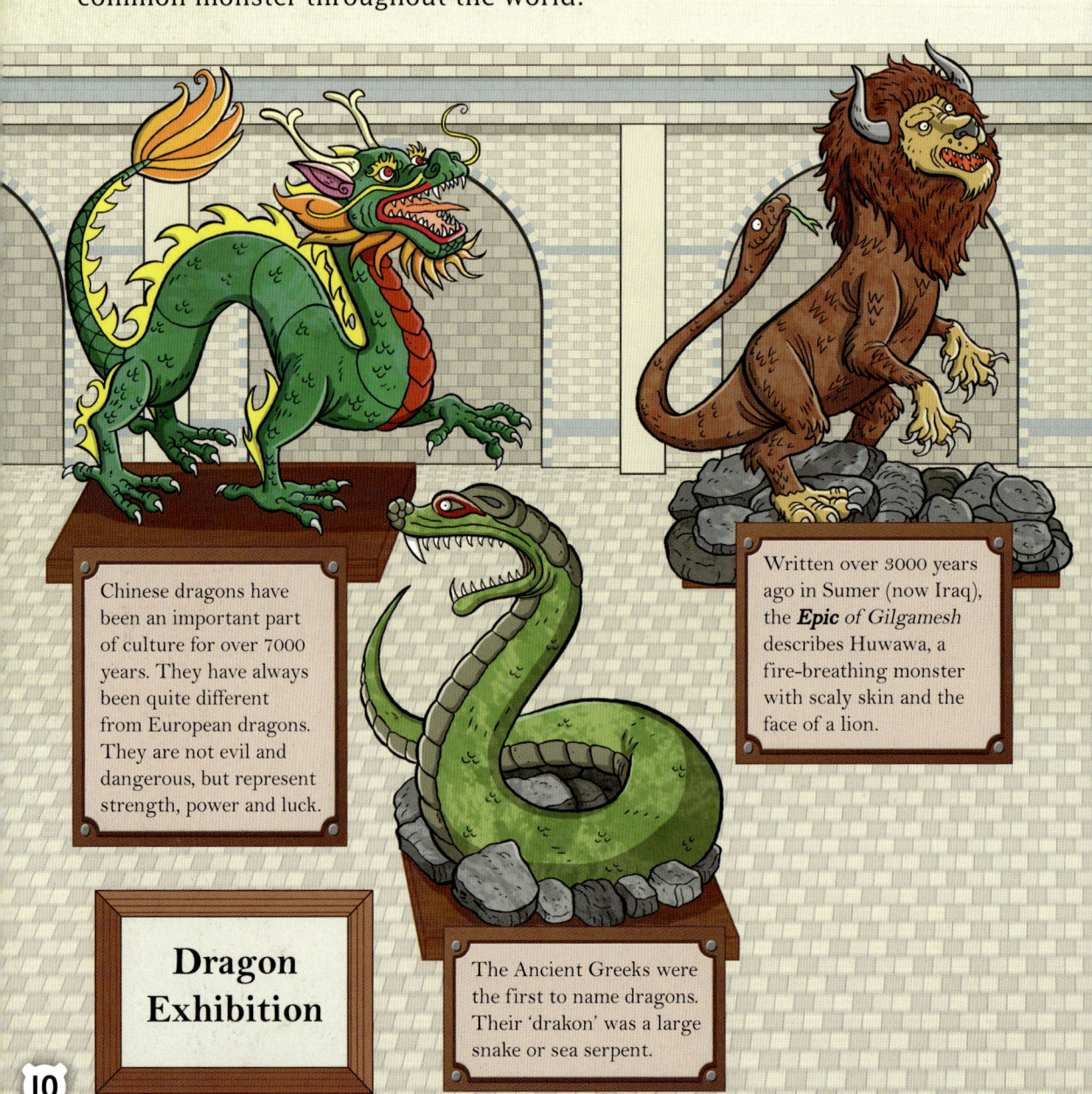

Chinese dragons have been an important part of culture for over 7000 years. They have always been quite different from European dragons. They are not evil and dangerous, but represent strength, power and luck.

Written over 3000 years ago in Sumer (now Iraq), the **Epic** of Gilgamesh describes Huwawa, a fire-breathing monster with scaly skin and the face of a lion.

The Ancient Greeks were the first to name dragons. Their 'drakon' was a large snake or sea serpent.

Dragon Exhibition

Other common monsters

The undead
In traditional tales, fearful monsters could also represent the spirits of dead people that had returned to seek revenge. In Viking **sagas**, *draugrs* or *attegangars* were the scariest monsters. In the old Norse language, *attegangar* means 'one who walks again'. *Draugrs* were the spirit guardians who protected the tombs of dead Vikings. Important Viking **chieftains** were buried with their treasure, so terrifying stories about *draugrs* may have helped to keep away grave robbers.

Frightful fairies
Monsters don't have to be big: people once feared fairies. They believed these mythical creatures swapped human babies for fairy children. In Scandinavia there was a tradition that fairy folk were afraid of iron so superstitious parents left a knife or a pair of scissors in a baby's bed as protection!

Dragons in medieval Europe were thought to look like lizards with wings.

In Ancient Egyptian stories, the god Apep appeared as a snake and, later, a dragon.

What's in a name?
So why did so many different people, on opposite sides of the world, tell the same type of monstery tales? Perhaps because they shared the same fears, too. Turning these fears into stories – and naming the 'monsters' – may have made them seem less frightening.

Alien Invaders

Today most people agree that it's foolish to fear monsters because they don't exist. However, a surprising number of people are frightened by something else which we have no proof exists: aliens from outer space. Fear of aliens is more widespread than you might think. Where might this fear come from?

DAILY NEWS

FIRST EDITION — **12TH JUNE**

OUT OF THIS WORLD!

A 2002 poll suggested that nearly half of the American people believed that aliens had visited the earth in UFOs (unidentified flying objects). Although it contained no evidence that they existed, the poll suggested that aliens had kidnapped nearly four million Americans.

Fear of the unknown

In the past, the word 'alien' just meant foreign and different. People feared invasions of strangers with different customs who might change their way of life. A thousand years ago, the 'aliens' were Viking fighters who terrorized northern Europe. Three centuries later, **Mongol** warriors caused the same fear. These fearsome strangers had deadly reputations and people often fled their homes and villages to escape them.

Fear of space aliens could be considered a modern version of this age-old fear. The Internet is jam-packed with tales of alien encounters and for many the threat may seem real, even if they have never seen an alien in real life. In 1938, this fear caused mass panic ...

War of the Worlds

In 1938 a radio drama described an attack on New York City by aliens from Mars. It was scripted to sound just like a real news programme and many people who tuned in after the start believed an alien invasion really had begun.

> Ladies and gentlemen, this is the most terrifying thing I have ever witnessed ... Wait a minute! Someone's crawling out of the hollow top. Someone or ... something. I can see peering out of that black hole two luminous disks ... are they eyes? It might be a face. It might be ...

An extract from the script of 'War of the Worlds.'

Thousands of listeners panicked and fled the city, jamming the roads with traffic. Hundreds of people rang *The New York Times* newspaper, and one caller asked "What time will it be the end of the world?"

New York's alien invaders existed only in the mind of the play's director, Orson Welles.

Light and Dark

Step out into the sunlight and bask in the warmth. Doesn't it feel good? Now imagine what it would be like if the Sun vanished forever. In the shivering, dark world plants wouldn't grow and, before long, every living thing would die. Now that's scary!

For much of human history, people knew very little about the Sun and they had a genuine fear that one morning it might not rise. Different **civilizations** devised different ceremonies and festivals which they believed would prevent the Sun's disappearance.

Aztec gore-fest

The Aztec people of Mexico worshipped the Sun as a god. They called their sun god *Ipalnemohuani,* meaning 'he that gives life'. They believed the Sun would stop rising unless they carried out human **sacrifices**.

Warning – this bit is grisly! At the top of vast pyramids in Tenochtitlán (now Mexico City), Aztec priests used razor-sharp stone knives to cut open the chests of prisoners, pulling out the still-beating hearts and offering them to the Sun. Up to 50 000 sacrifices were made every year to please the sun god.

Aztec priests threw sacrificed prisoners down the steep steps of the pyramid after cutting out their hearts.

The sun in danger

When the Sun slipped out of sight at dusk each day, Egyptian people believed it entered the **underworld**, a dark place of great danger. Priests offered prayers and ceremonies to make sure that the Sun rose safely again in the morning. Egyptians believed in several sun gods and their city of Heliopolis, built 4600 years ago, was named after the Sun and dedicated to its worship.

A brilliant sun disc shone from the head of hawk-faced Egyptian Sun god Ra-Harakhty.

An underworld god tries to catch and eat people's shadows.

Save our shadows

On the Indonesian island of Nias, people believed that the sun god Lowalangi owned all humans and gave them their shadows. Priests performed **rituals** to show respect to the Sun and to ensure that people kept their shadows.

Truth behind the fear

Fears about the Sun faltering or failing were a common theme throughout history. Today we know that they were not completely foolish. Scientists agree that the Sun, like all stars, will eventually die, burning up the Earth in the process. The good news? This won't happen for a billion years or more.

The Sun Eaten Up

Although the Sun won't disappear any time soon, an eclipse can make it vanish temporarily. Even when **astronomers** discovered how eclipses occurred, ordinary people still feared them: they believed that eclipses foretold disaster.

Truth behind the fear

A solar eclipse happens when the Moon moves between the Earth and the Sun. The Moon's shadow races across the Earth's surface, blocking out the Sun. It briefly turns day into night.

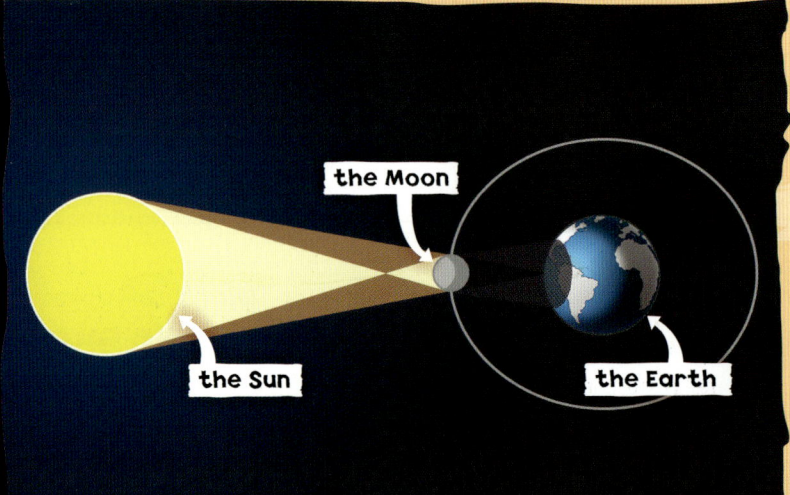

Eclipses around the world

- The Vikings believed that solar eclipses happened when a hungry wolf chased the Sun across the sky, caught it and ate it. They thought they could scare off the wolf – and bring back the Sun – by making a lot of noise during an eclipse.

- The Ancient Chinese believed an eclipse began when a dragon tried to eat the Sun. Even now, the Chinese word for eclipse is *riquanshi*, which means 'the Sun completely eaten'.

- The Native American Ojibway people fired flaming arrows at the eclipsed Sun to relight it. They believed this rescued them all from everlasting night.

Using foolish fears

The Greek **philosopher** Thales was the first person to accurately forecast an eclipse, in 585 BC. His predicted eclipse ended a battle:

> **Both Lydians and Medes broke off from fighting when they saw this darkening of the day: they were more anxious to make peace.**
>
> Greek historian Herodotus, writing about 150 years after the battle.

In 1503, Italian explorer Christopher Columbus used fear of lunar eclipses to trick Caribbean islanders into feeding his hungry crew. He told the local people that angry gods would turn the Moon red and he warned them when it would happen. When the Moon darkened, the terrified islanders gave him what he needed.

Fear factor

As many as 2000 years ago, Chinese astronomers understood and predicted eclipses. But before this, astronomers sometimes paid a high price for inaccurate forecasts. In 2300 BC two astronomers who got it wrong had their heads cut off!

Fear of the Dark

An extreme fear of the dark is known as *nyctophobia*. Luckily for modern sufferers, light is always there at the flick of a switch – but it wasn't always like this.

Fear factor

Electric lighting was invented in the 1880s. Dim gas lighting became available only 80 years earlier. Before that, candles and fires cast dim circles of light but the night hid everything else in inky blackness.

Before gas and electric lighting, fear of the dark wasn't so foolish for darkness really *did* hide danger. On a moonless night, dangers that were ordinary and easy to avoid by day became deathtraps. In cities, travellers risked falling into piles of rubbish or open cellars. In the countryside, pits, rivers and mineshafts waited to swallow those who walked out on dark nights.

Truth behind the fear

When people lived in caves and camps, those who strayed from the fireside at night risked being eaten by hungry animals. People who feared darkness survived and passed on their cautious attitude to their children.

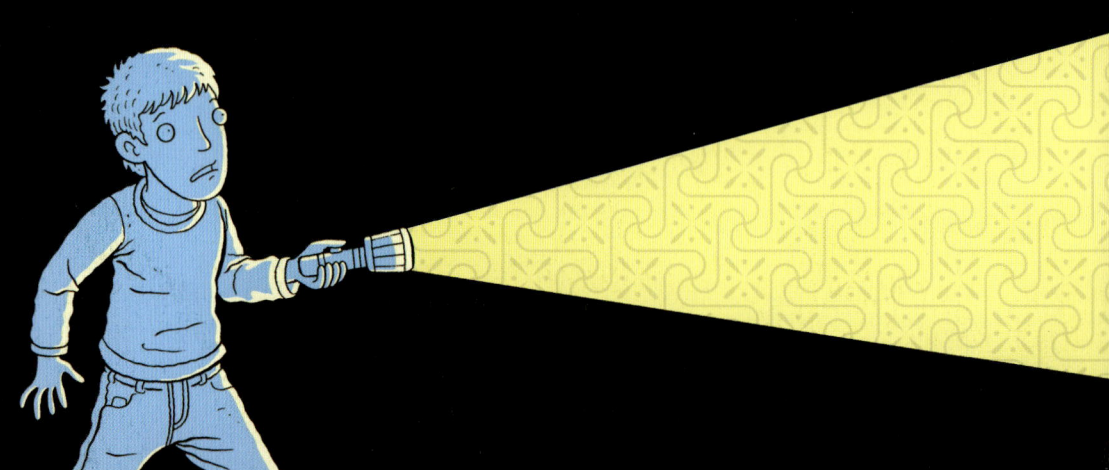

Night-time hides the villains

Before streetlights made cities safer, thieves could lurk in the darkness. They camouflaged themselves and wore dark clothes, becoming invisible. Some threatened to kill their victims in order to take their money.

Fear factor

People living in the countryside believed in glowing spirits called jack-o'-lanterns or will-o'-the-wisps, which lured travellers off the safe path.

Things that go bump in the night

Many people are still afraid of the dark, even when there is nothing real to fear. There is plenty to imagine if you are nervous. When the Sun sets, our imaginations play tricks on us and ominous shadows seem to lurk round every corner.

Moon-phase discs on grandfather clocks like this one were not just pretty decorations: travellers used them to judge whether the Moon would provide enough light to make a safe night-time journey.

YOUR DESTINY IN THE STARS

Do you think that the position of the planets affects your fate? Five hundred years ago, almost everybody took **astrology** *very* seriously. People sought advice from astrologers before planting crops, treating illnesses or making journeys.

The Toledo letter

In 1184 the Pope and many other high-ranking people received a message of doom, apparently from astronomers in Toledo, Spain. They warned that in September of that year, the positions of the planets would cause storms, famine, disease and earthquakes that would destroy the world.

The prediction was taken very seriously. A religious leader in England told his followers to starve themselves for three days which he said would prevent disaster. The dreaded date arrived – and nothing happened.

Predicting a flood

Astrologers calculated that in February 1524 the Earth and the Sun would line up with the planets Mercury, Venus, Mars, Jupiter and Saturn. They said this would cause torrential rain and flooding.

Drowning in a drought

In London there was actually a drought but 20 000 terrified people fled their homes anyway.

A real-life ark

Meanwhile, in Germany, wealthy Count von Iggleheim built a three-storey luxury ship on the River Rhine. On the predicted day in 1524 he went on board to escape drowning. Crowds gathered on the bank to laugh at him. However, when a few drops of rain fell, panic grew. When the Count refused to let anybody else on board his ship, he was pulled ashore and stoned to death. The rain stopped soon afterwards.

This image was created at the time of the prediction and shows the prophesied rain and floods.

The rain is not the only thing you need to worry about – watch your hand.

Mark my words, the rain will start soon!

Truth behind the fear

Today we can rely on science and accurate information when planning our lives and most people just read **horoscopes** for amusement. However, some people still rely on astrology for guidance when making important decisions.

Stars with Fiery Tails

Scientists have learnt a great deal about comets – they've been studying them for over 500 years and have even photographed them in outer space. But these 'dirty snowballs' were once thought of as fiery messengers, warning of doom, defeat or destruction.

Halley's comet

The most famous comet can be seen from Earth every 75 years. It is named after the astronomer Edmond Halley – in 1705 he was the first to predict its regular return. Until his studies, the comet caused alarm every time it appeared, often being linked to unfortunate events. In 1066 it showed up just before a French army defeated the English king. It reappeared in 1222, just before Mongol armies began to attack Europe.

> **"** This comet was so horrible, so frightful, and it produced such great terror among the common people, that many died of fear and many others fell sick. **"**
>
> French surgeon Ambrose Paré, writing about a comet that passed close to Earth in 1528.

Truth behind the fear

Speeding through space, comets are actually balls of ice and dust that can be seen when they pass close to Earth.

Halley's comet

The Bayeux Tapestry is a 70 m-long strip of fabric sewn with pictures. It tells the story of the 1066 Norman invasion of England. In one scene, Frenchmen point to the comet that predicts their victory.

Gas panic

In 1910 the Earth passed right through the tail of Halley's comet as the two orbits crossed. Astronomers warned that poisonous gases in the tail "would ... possibly snuff out all life on the planet". In Istanbul, Turkey, parents kept their children out of school for the day so that the whole family would be together should the end come. Frightened Americans bought gas masks and sealed up their rooms to escape the danger. In fact, the comet was harmless.

Truth behind the fear

Fear of speeding space rocks isn't entirely foolish. 65 million years ago a huge **asteroid** hit Mexico's Yucatán region; the smash is thought to have killed off the dinosaurs. It could happen again – but it's very unlikely.

Fear factor

Halley's comet wasn't the only one to cause foolish fears. In 1556, German King Charles V was so scared by a comet that he gave up his crown and became a monk!

Mother Nature and Angry Gods

Ancient Greeks were so afraid of their goat-legged god Pan that they named their greatest fear after him: 'panic' means a sudden, overwhelming feeling of terror. It's a reminder that, in the past, the gods were the most frightening things of all.

Ancient people often worshipped many different gods. Some gods were guardians who looked after humans but others had a terrifying side, threatening to harm them. For the people who believed in them, the gods were a way of making sense of a world that sometimes seemed cruel and unfair. When storms, earthquakes, floods or volcanoes caused chaos, ancient peoples blamed their gods and prayed to them for mercy.

Vulcan

Romans named volcanoes after this important god, thought of as a metalworker armed with thunderbolts. When Vulcan was angry, fearful worshippers tried to calm him down by throwing fish into a fire.

Mafui'e

In Samoa, the earthquake god Mafui'e was also an **underworld** god of fire.

Nuba

In Chinese folk religion, Nuba was the goddess of drought. When rain had not fallen, people held ceremonies that would drive her away so that wet weather would return.

Tlaloc

The Aztec people of Mexico worshipped the fertility god Tlaloc. They believed he made their crops grow but they also feared his power. If Tlaloc was angry, he would send torrential rain, lightning and thunder. The Aztecs thought that **sacrificing** children would calm his fury.

Inkanyamba

To the Zulu people of South Africa, Inkanyamba was a serpent god with a horse's head, who lived in the region's waterfalls. Inkanyamba created violent and destructive summer tornadoes.

Pan

Though Pan's mischievous calls frightened people in lonely places, he wasn't really an evil god. He enjoyed music and dancing and is said to have invented the pipes named after him.

WHAT DOESN'T KILL YOU MAKES YOU STRONGER

Until a few hundred years ago, diseases were truly terrifying. Doctors knew almost nothing about the real causes of illness and the only tools they could use to **diagnose** patients were guesswork, studying patients' wee and poo, and experience. Some doctors even relied on astrology (see page 20).

A deadly cure?
In medieval Europe, whatever disease had been diagnosed, the most likely treatment was bloodletting (cutting a vein open to let some blood flow out of the body). This never cured patients and often killed them. Anyone lucky enough to survive this dangerous treatment believed the doctor had cured them, so bloodletting continued. The treatment was popular well into the 19th century, when **leeches** were often used to suck blood from the body.

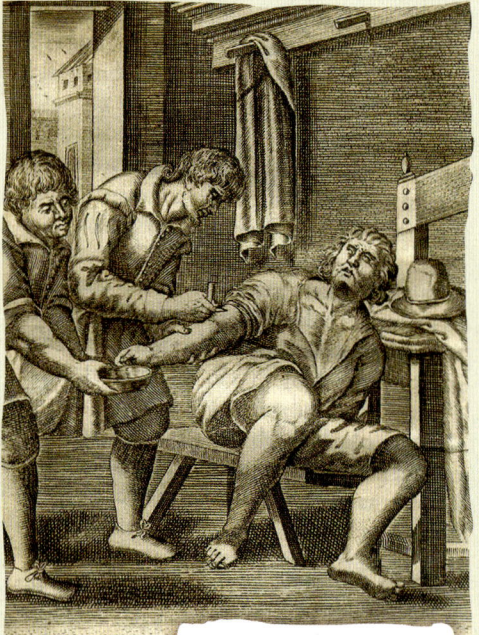

When they drained patients' blood, doctors used number puzzles and star charts to decide which vein to cut open.

Truth behind the fear
It's natural and normal to fear illness, injury and disease. After all, they bring pain and suffering, and perhaps even death. Modern medicine means we have less to fear than at any time in the past. **Vaccinations** stop us from catching many diseases but diseases mutate and it's a challenge for even modern medicine to keep up. Outbreaks of deadly disease still cause fear and panic.

Folk remedies

In the past, poor people couldn't afford to pay doctors' fees. Although their home-made treatments were little better at healing than bloodletting, they were usually less deadly. Can you guess what these foolish treatments were for? (Answers down the sides!)

rheumatism: Sleep next to a dog and it will take the illness over from you.

boils: Rub the skin with the hair of a grey male horse.

a bad cold: Hang a sock full of roast potatoes round your neck.

gout: Carry the right foot of a frog, wrapped in deerskin.

whooping cough: Drink water from a bishop's skull, or breathe in a cow's breath.

shingles: Smear the affected area with blood from the tail of a black cat.

warts: Touch each affected body part with a different stone. Put the stones in a bag and drop them. Whoever picks up the stones will suffer the same illness and you will be cured.

Bad Smells and Disease

When **epidemics** swept across Europe in the Middle Ages, people fled in terror. One of the worst was the Black Death, a deadly outbreak of a disease called bubonic plague, which killed up to half of Europe's people in the mid-14th century. People were right to fear the Black Death but, foolishly, they blamed bad smells for spreading it.

What a pong!

At the time, nobody really knew how diseases spread. However, they noticed that people who lived in dirty, smelly conditions were more likely to die, so they linked bad smells to disease and tried to protect themselves by sniffing bundles of sweet herbs. In fact, the herbs gave no protection: the cause of plague was not odours but bites from fleas that carried the disease.

Bad air

Plague is not the only disease once linked to bad smells. Malaria gets its name from the Italian words *mala* (bad) and *aria* (air) because it was common near foul-smelling swamps. Odours took the blame until 1897, when Scottish doctor Ronald Ross discovered that it was the mosquitoes living in swamp water that spread malaria.

Fear factor

The idea that bad smells caused disease was called 'miasma theory'. Germs were not discovered until the 19th century.

Let's get out of here!

The Black Death killed more people in cities than in the countryside. To try and escape the disease, fearful rich people moved to their country houses. However, in doing so they took the disease with them and spread it nationwide. Poor city-dwellers were just as scared but they had nowhere to go. They died in their thousands.

> **The plague spread so thickly that the living were hardly able to bury the dead.**
>
> Thomas Walsingham, a monk of St Albans, 1390.

Terrifying bells

The plague returned to London in the 17th century, killing so many people that the bodies were collected in handcarts. At first, those pushing the carts rang bells to warn the healthy but the constant ringing frightened so many people that they stopped.

Truth behind the fear

Some bad smells really *can* kill you. Many volcanoes release sulphur dioxide, a gas that smells strongly of bad eggs. Sniff enough of it and you could have difficulty breathing and eventually die.

Doctors looking after plague victims wore beak-shaped masks with herbs tucked in the nose and they only touched their patients with wooden sticks.

THE EDGE OF THE EARTH

Some 2350 years ago, Greek traveller Pytheas sailed north of Britain. On the sixth day of the voyage, he saw something extraordinary. The sea and sky seemed joined together. A fisherman told him it was the edge of the world and that he should turn back. Fearful of what lay beyond, Pytheas sailed for home.

Today, people don't fear the edge of the world as Pytheas did. We know that the Earth has no end or edge: it's round, like a football so if you travel far enough in a straight line you will end up where you started. However, thousands of years ago the fear of falling off the edge of the Earth was common among many. After all, people couldn't see photographs of Earth from space as we can today.

Truth behind the fear

Pytheas had probably sailed so far north that the sea was frozen to slush. If fog hid the **horizon** from view, ocean and sky would seem to merge.

Most scholars have known the Earth is ball-shaped for over 2500 years but not everyone was convinced. This engraving shows a traveller on an Earth that is flat like a dinner-plate.

The sailor's clue

Sailors were some of the first people to work out that the Earth is not flat. If it was, then departing ships would just look smaller the farther they sail from shore. In fact, they gradually sink below the horizon as well as appearing to shrink.

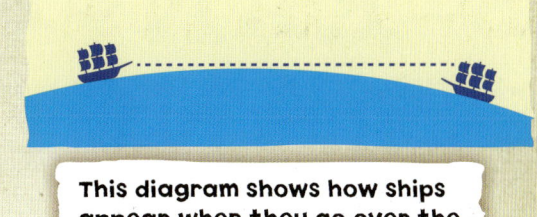

This diagram shows how ships appear when they go over the horizon line.

Crossing the Atlantic

When Italian explorer Christopher Columbus led the first European voyage across the mid-Atlantic in 1492, his Spanish sailors were terrified. Though they did not believe the world was flat, they were frightened because they thought they would never see their families again. Were these foolish fears or not? What do you think?

> I am having serious trouble with the crew, complaining they will never be able to return home. They have said that it is insanity and suicidal to risk their lives following the madness of a foreigner. Some feel that they have already arrived where men have never dared to sail, and that they are not obliged to go to the end of the world.

Columbus's diary entry for Monday 24th September 1492, 4000 km from home.

STRANGE PEOPLE, STRANGE LANDS

More than 2000 years ago, historians from Ancient Rome wrote about the savage people of a distant country. One wrote that "they plunge into swamps and live there for many days with only their heads above water". Another said that these people went everywhere naked, painted their skin blue and tattooed themselves with pictures of wild beasts. Where did these fearsome 'savages' live? In England!

Most of these descriptions were just foolish fantasies. The Roman historians had not visited the places they wrote about they based their stories on rumours and legends. However, since there were no better descriptions, people believed what they read. As travellers began to explore the world, they feared meeting such weird and alarming peoples.

Truth behind the fear

Roman historians got at least one thing right. Ancient Britons really *did* paint their skin blue, to make themselves more fearsome in battle. They used the juice of a plant called woad as a dye.

Monsters on maps

Roman historian Pliny wrote equally foolish stories about people who lived in Africa. For instance, he said the king of one African tribe had a single eye in the middle of his forehead and that another tribe "... have heads like those of dogs". Map-makers believed Pliny's descriptions, because they had no other evidence of what African people were really like. For the next thousand years they drew these imaginary monsters on their maps of Africa.

Ancient map-makers who drew imaginary people in Africa knew no better. Until 150 years ago, Europeans had explored only the coasts and the rivers of Africa.

Man or beast?

It wasn't just travellers who were frightened of meeting people from distant lands. When Spanish conqueror Hernando Cortés arrived in Central America in 1519, his armoured knights terrified the native people. They had never seen horses before and thought that each four-legged beast and its rider was a single animal with two heads. Even when the riders dismounted, the native people still believed the horse was a fierce enemy.

FOOLISHLY FAST?

People have always been frightened of new, faster forms of travel, as these examples show.

Speedy stagecoaches

Fears about travelling fast began long before the **Industrial Revolution**: even fast horse-drawn coaches were too much for nervous types. In 1784 a new **stagecoach** cut the journey time between London and Bath from three days to 17 hours. A worried doctor wrote that:

Two-horsepower is too much for me!

> Regular travel at such **prodigious** speeds must surely result in death.

Steam fiends

Until the invention of steam trains in the 1830s the fastest way to travel was on the back of a galloping horse, so this new form of transport seemed dangerously fast. English professor Dionysus Lardner advised that:

Oh golly!

> Rail travel at high speed is not possible because passengers, unable to breathe, would die of **asphyxia**.

How fast were these steam fiends going? A leisurely 45 kilometres per hour!

Horseless carriages

When the first cars appeared on the roads around 60 years later, they caused similar alarm. Riders and coach travellers feared that the noise, speed and smell of these 'horseless carriages' would panic their horses. The government took swift action and passed a law that cars could travel no faster than six kilometres per hour on country roads and half that speed in towns!

Blast off!

Speed terror continued into the 20th century. In 1936, when the invention of powerful rockets made space travel a distant possibility, surgeon John Lockhart Mummery wrote that:

> The acceleration which must result from the use of rockets ... would damage the brain beyond repair.

Fear or thrill?

A few of us get scared by every advance in transport technology; it's our natural fear of the new and unknown. But for others, speed is a thrilling, joyful experience: just ask anyone queuing at a theme park for a white-knuckle ride!

Truth behind the fear

We may laugh at people in the past who feared fast travel, but with the powerful cars of today, it's a sensible fear. A person travelling in a car at 80 kilometres per hour is 20 times more likely to die in a crash than one travelling at 30 kilometres per hour.

CAN FEAR BE HELPFUL?

Everyone knows what fear feels like. Your heart beats faster. You sweat. You look nervously over your shoulder. You get ready to run – or fight for your life. Does this mean fear is a bad feeling?

No! All these changes make you more ready to react to danger. Fear helps you survive.

What about foolish fears?

Sometimes we *know* there isn't any real danger but the fear feels real nonetheless. Blame it on our ancestors. They lived in a world where deadly animals roamed freely and the people who felt fear most keenly were more likely to avoid being eaten; this fear got passed down through the generations. Thousands of years later our cities are free of large, hungry animals but our inherited fear still remains.

The feeling of fear

The physical changes that you experience when you are frightened are caused by **adrenalin**. This is a natural chemical that your brain makes in response to fear. It helps prepare your body to face danger. As your heart beats faster, more blood is pumped to your legs so that you have more energy to run to safety.

Making the right decision

Fear helps us in another, less dramatic way. When we have to make a quick decision, a little fear can help guide us away from the wrong choice. Experiments have shown that we sometimes make better decisions when we don't think carefully about the result. When time is short we have to trust our instincts – fear is one of the most basic and powerful instincts we have.

Thrill seekers

Sometimes feeling fear can be fun! Many of us like riding roller-coasters that make us scream out loud. And some people queue to watch scary movies at the cinema. Why do we choose to be frightened? **Psychologists** say it's because we like to face and overcome fear; the make-believe risk excites us and we can enjoy the adrenalin rush without the real danger.

FUTURE FEARS

Fears have changed over time according to the dangers life holds. Have you ever thought about what people in the future might fear? There will always be something to fear, even if it's just fear itself.

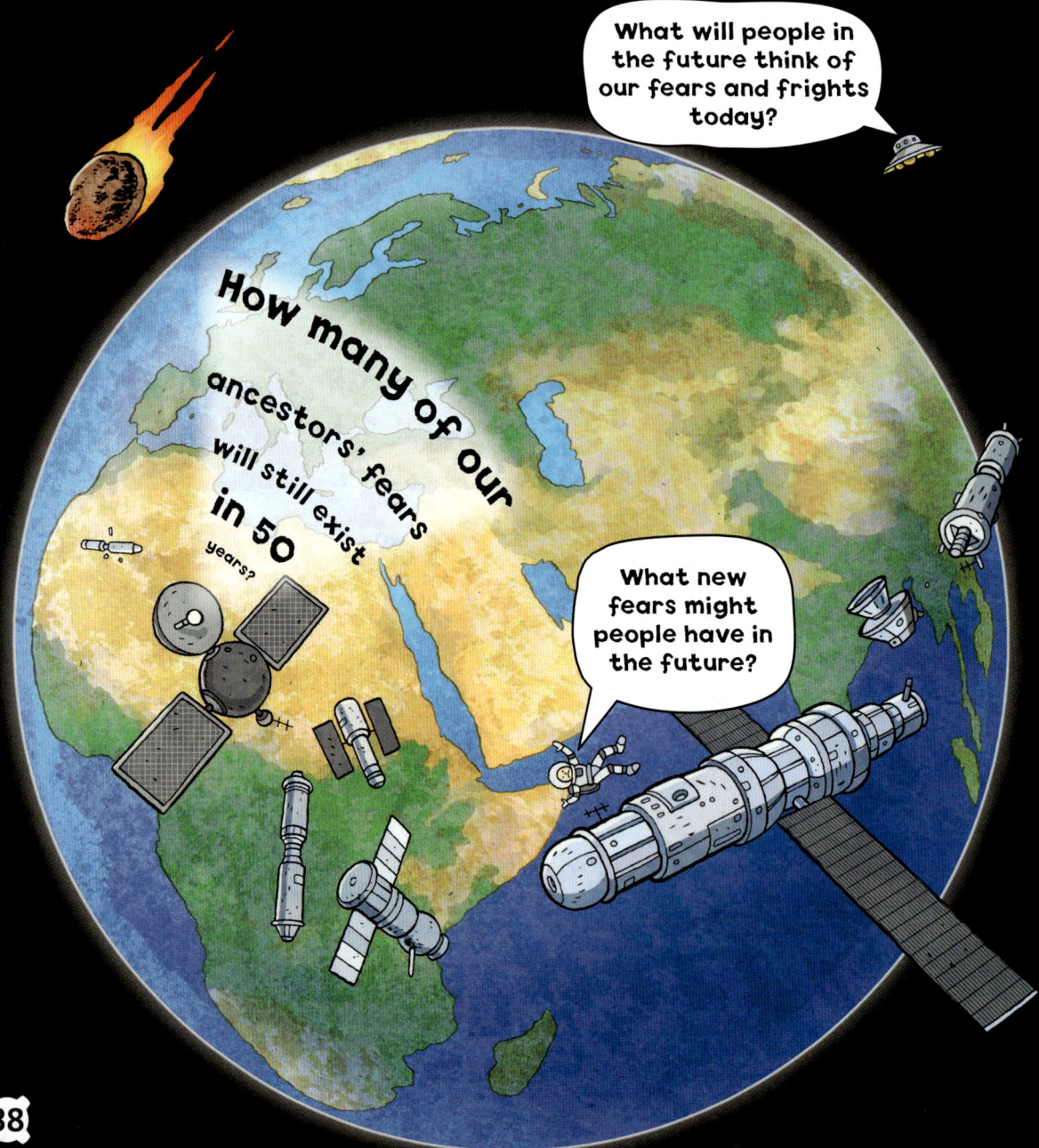

GLOSSARY

adrenalin — a chemical released from our bodies in stressful situations

ancestor — someone's parents, grandparents, great-grandparents, and so on, through to the most distant members of a family

asphyxia — the removal of air or breathing, eventually causing death

assassin — a murderer, especially one paid to kill an important person

asteroid — a small lump of rock circling a star or sun

astrology — prediction of future events, by studying the positions of the planets

astronomer — someone who studies the science of the stars and planets

chieftain — the leader of a group or tribe

civilization — a particular culture or way of life

diagnose — to identify a disease by its symptoms

epic — a long poem of adventures and great deeds, especially one that was memorized and spoken before being written down

epidemic — a serious outbreak of a disease in which many people fall ill or die

horizon — a distant line where the sky meets the sea or land

horoscope — an astrologer's guess at what the future holds for someone, based on the date of their birth

Industrial Revolution — the period of rapid development in the 18th and 19th centuries using new or improved machinery rather than manual labour

leech — a bloodsucking worm used in the past to draw blood for medicinal reasons

Mongol — the people of Mongolia, who conquered China in 1215

pagan — the name given by Christians in the past to those who did not share their religion

philosopher — an expert who uses reason and argument in seeking the truth, often interested in why we exist

prime number — a number that can only be divided by itself and one

prodigious — unusually great in size or ability

psychologist — a scientist who studies the human mind

ritual — special actions repeated in a strict order, often as part of a religious service

sacrifice — the killing of an animal or person as part of a religious celebration

saga — a collection of traditional stories, specifically from Iceland or Norway

stagecoach — a horse-drawn coach that ran to a regular timetable

underworld — an imaginary place beneath the ground where the dead live again

vaccination — injection of a weakened form of a disease that provides someone with protection against the disease itself

vestments — clothing

INDEX

agoraphobia 3
aliens 12–13
asteroids.. 23
astrology 20–1
astronomy 17
Aztecs................................... 14, 25
Black Death 28–29
China 10, 17, 25
Columbus, Christopher........... 17, 31
comets 22–23
darkness...................... 2, 14, 18–19
disease................................... 26–29
death 8, 26, 28–29
doctors 26, 29
dragons 10–11, 17
dreams................................... 8–9
drowning 21
eclipses................................. 16–17
Egypt 6, 7, 15
fairies 11
flat earth.......................... 30–31
Greece............... 6, 10, 17, 24, 25, 30
gods................. 7, 11, 14–15, 24–25
horoscopes........................... 21

legends 10–11, 2
lighting 18
luck................................... 4–7
magical beliefs 5
Mongols 12, 22
monsters 10–11, 32–33
Moon................................ 16, 19
night 16, 18–19
nightmares 8–9
numbers 7
panic................................. 24, 25
phobias................................. 3
plague............................ 28–29
planets............................ 20–21
Romans....................... 7, 24, 32–33
sacrifice 14, 25
smells 28–29
speed 34–35
Sun............................ 14–17, 21
superstitions 4–7
travel 31, 34–35
underworld.................... 15, 24
Vikings 11, 12
white-knuckle rides............ 34, 37

> **Page 3 Name that fear – answers**
> chromophobia – fear of bright colours; dentophobia – fear of dentists; bibliophobia – fear of books; frigophobia – fear of getting cold; zoophobia – fear of animals; hippophobia – fear of horses